THE
PASSIONATE
LIFE

BIBLE STUDY SERIES

Ephesians
HEAVEN'S
RICHES

12-WEEK STUDY GUIDE

BroadStreet
P U B L I S H I N G

BroadStreet Publishing Group, LLC
Racine, Wisconsin, USA
BroadStreetPublishing.com

The Passionate Life Bible Study Series
EPHESIANS: HEAVEN'S RICHES 12-WEEK STUDY GUIDE

Copyright © 2016 The Passion Translation®

Edited by Jeremy Bouma

ISBN-13: 978-1-4245-5333-4 (soft cover)
ISBN-13: 978-1-4245-5334-1 (e-book)

To purchase any of the study guides in the The Passionate Life Bible Study Series in bulk for use in groups, please send an email to orders@broadstreetpublishing.com.

Cover design by Chris Garborg at GarborgDesign.com
Typesetting by Katherine Lloyd at theDESKonline.com

Printed in the United States of America

16 17 18 19 20 5 4 3 2 1

Contents

Using The Passionate Life Bible Study

The psalmist declares, "Truth's shining light guides me in my choices and decisions; the revelation of your Word makes my pathway clear" (Psalm 119:105).

This verse forms the foundation of The Passionate Life Bible Study series. Not only do we want to kindle within you a deep, burning passion for God and his Word, but we also want to let the Word's light blaze a bright path before you to help you make truth-filled choices and decisions, while encountering the heart of God along the way.

God longs to have his Word expressed in a way that unlocks the passion of his heart for the reader. Inspired by The Passion Translation but usable with any Bible translation, this is a heart-level Bible study, from the passion of God's heart to the passion of your heart. Our goal is to trigger inside you an over-whelming response to the truth of the Bible.

DISCOVER. EXPLORE. EXPERIENCE. SHARE.

Each of the following lessons is divided into four sections: *Discover the Heart of God*; *Explore the Heart of God*; *Experience the Heart of God*; and *Share the Heart of God*. They are meant to guide your study of the truth of God's Word, while drawing you closer and deeper into his passionate heart for you and your world.

The *Discover* section is designed to help you make observations about the reading. Every lesson opens with the same three questions: What did you notice, perhaps for the first time? What questions do you have? And, what did you learn about the heart of God? There are no right answers here! They are meant to jump-start your journey into God's truth by bringing to the surface your initial impressions about the passage. The other questions help draw your attention to specific points the author wrote and discover the truths God is conveying.

Explore takes you deeper into God's Word by inviting you to think more critically and explain what the passage is saying. Often there is some extra information to highlight and clarify certain aspects of the passage, while inviting you to make connections. Don't worry if the answers aren't immediately apparent. Sometimes you may need to dig a little deeper or take a little more time to think. You'll be grateful you did, because you will have tapped into God's revelation-light in greater measure!

Experience is meant to help you do just that: experience God's heart for you personally. It will help you live out God's Word by applying it to your unique life situation. Each question in this section is designed to bring the Bible into your world in fresh, exciting, and relevant ways. At the end of this section, you will have a better idea of how to make choices and decisions that please God, while walking through life on clear paths bathed in the light of his revelation!

The final section is *Share*. God's Word isn't meant to be merely studied or memorized; it's meant to be shared with other people—both through living and telling. This section helps you understand how the reading relates to growing closer to others, to enriching your fellowship and relationship with your world. It also helps you listen to the stories of those around you, so you can bridge Jesus' story with their stories.

SUGGESTIONS FOR INDIVIDUAL STUDY

Reading and studying the Bible is an exciting journey! This study is designed to help you encounter the heart of God and let his Word to you reach deep down into your very soul—all so you can live and enjoy the life he intends for you. And like with any journey, a number of practices will help you along the way:

1. Begin your lesson time in prayer, asking God to open up his Word to you in new ways, show areas of your heart that need teaching

and healing, and correct any area in which you're living contrary to his desires for your life.

2. Read the opening section to gain an understanding of the major themes of the reading and ideas for each lesson.

3. Read through the Scripture passage once, underlining or noting in your Bible anything that stands out to you. Reread the passage again, keeping in mind these three questions: What did you notice, perhaps for the first time? What questions do you have? What did you learn about the heart of God?

4. Write your answers to the questions in this Bible study guide or a notebook. If you do get stuck, first ask God to reveal his Word to you and guide you in his truth. And then, either wait until your small group time or ask a trusted leader for help.

5. Use the end of the lesson to focus your time of prayer, thanking and praising God for the truth of his Word, for what he has revealed to you, and for how he has impacted your daily life.

SUGGESTIONS FOR SMALL GROUP STUDY

The goal of this study is to understand God's Word for you and your community in greater measure, while encountering his heart along the way. A number of practices will help your group as you journey together:

1. Group studies usually go better when everyone is prepared to participate. The best way to prepare is to come having read the lesson's Scripture reading beforehand. Following the suggestions in each individual study will enrich your time as a community as well.

2. Before you begin the study, your group should nominate a leader to guide the discussion. While this person should work through the questions beforehand, his or her main job isn't to lecture, but to

help move the conversation along by asking the lesson questions and facilitating the discussion.

3. Encourage everyone to share. Be sure to listen well, contribute where you feel led, and try not to dominate the conversation.

4. The number one rule for community interaction is: nothing is off-limits! No question is too dumb; no answer is out of bounds. While many questions in this study have "right" answers, most are designed to push you and your friends to explore the passage more deeply and understand what it means for daily living.

5. Finally, be ready for God to reveal himself through the passage being discussed and through the discussion that arises out of the group he's put together. Pray that he would reveal his heart and revelation-light to you all in deeper ways. And be open to being challenged, corrected, and changed.

Again, we pray and trust that this Bible study will kindle in you a burning, passionate desire for God and his heart, while impacting your life for years to come. May it open wide the storehouse of heaven's revelation-light. May it reveal new and greater insights into the mysteries of God and the king-dom-realm life he has for you. And may you encounter the heart of God in more fresh and relevant ways than you ever thought possible!

Introduction to Ephesians

What you are about to explore is the very constitution of our faith, the great summary description of all that is precious and esteemed in Christian doctrine and Christian living. Paul firmly planted the cornerstone of our faith in this powerful letter, bringing before every believer the mystery of the glory of Christ.

What an exciting letter Paul has written to us! Ephesians is full of living revelation; it simply drips with the anointing of the Holy Spirit. Its theme is that God will one day submit everything under the lordship of Jesus Christ. Jesus is the Head of the church and the fullness of God in human flesh. He gives his church extraordinary power to walk filled with the Holy Spirit, revealing the nature of God in all things. Jesus loves the church and cherishes everything about her. The church is God's new humanity and the new temple where God's glory dwells. The church is also the Bride of Christ, the beloved partner that is destined to rule with him. How wonderfully he blesses his Bride with gifts from above, beginning with his matchless grace.

We've designed this study to help you discover and explore the greatness of God, which streams from Jesus Christ into the heart of every believer. Drink in the sweet riches of heaven's revelation, and enjoy diving deep into this most exhilarating letter from heaven. God is good to give the Holy Spirit's riches to those who ask with sincere hunger for more!

Lesson 1

___

Heaven's Lavish Love Gifts— Unsearchable and Ours!

EPHESIANS 1:1–14

Everything heaven contains has already been lavished upon us as a love gift from our wonderful heavenly Father, the Father of our Lord Jesus—all because he sees us wrapped into Christ. This is why we celebrate him with all our hearts! (Ephesians 1:3)

There is an old hymn that perfectly captures the essence of Paul's letter to the Ephesians. This is what you'll discover in this study: "Oh, the unsearchable riches of Christ; Wealth that can never be told! Riches exhaustless of mercy and grace; Precious, more precious than gold!"[1]

Unsearchable, precious riches indeed! Here's a glimpse from this lesson of those unsearchable riches: God chose us to be his very own, joining us to himself from creation; we are seen as holy, unstained, and innocent; through union with Christ, we are God's adoptive children; we've been given the treasures of salvation by the blood of Jesus—the total cancelation of our sins; the Holy Spirit himself has stamped and sealed us, guaranteeing these riches.

___

1. Frances J. Crosby, "Unsearchable Riches," 1882, public domain.

11

The remarkable revelation-truth that unfolds in this exploration of Ephesians is that all of heaven's lavish love gifts are already ours. The Holy Spirit has been "given to us like an engagement ring is given to a bride, as the first installment of what's coming!" (1:14). So drink in the sweet, unsearchable riches of heaven's revelation, and enjoy diving deep into this most exhilarating letter from heaven.

Discover the Heart of God

- After reading Ephesians 1:1–14, what did you notice, perhaps for the first time? What questions do you have? What did you learn about the heart of God?

- Why is it true that we have already received, as a lavish love gift, everything that heaven contains?

- Paul revealed that God chose us to be his very own. When and why did God do this?

- What did Paul reveal about God's plan to adopt us? What did he reveal about the nature of God's love?

- What did Paul say is powerfully working in us? What is the result, especially of being "joined to Christ"?

- What has the Holy Spirit done for everyone who is in Christ, both Jew and non-Jew? List a few of the benefits.

Explore the Heart of God

- What does it mean that "Everything heaven contains has already been lavished upon us as a love gift from our wonderful heavenly Father" (1:3)? What are these blessings, and how is this possible?

- What does it reveal about the heart of God that even before he created the world, he chose us to be his very own? What does it say about God's love for us that it is the same love he has for Jesus, the Anointed One?

- What does Paul mean by God's "superabundant grace" (1:8)? What is this?

- What were the secret desires and long-range plans of God that Paul speaks about in our reading? How does the Anointed One reveal them?

- Who is the Holy Spirit and why is he important? What does his ministry reveal about the heart of God?

Experience the Heart of God

- How does it make you feel to know that all of heaven's storehouses have already been lavishly poured out upon us?

- What does it mean for your experience of the heart of God to know that God chose you as his very own before you were born—even before the foundation of the world?

- Paul says that in God's eyes you are seen as holy, with an unstained innocence. And the same love he has for Jesus he has for you. Do you believe this? How might it affect your experience of the heart of God if you did?

- How have you seen God's "superabundant grace" powerfully at work in your life—guiding you, shaping you, caring for you?

- How should the knowledge that you've been sealed into relationship with the Holy Spirit and guaranteed an inheritance impact your experience of the heart of God?

Share the Heart of God

- Paul shares with us the delightful revelation-truth that God has chosen people from the foundation of the universe as his children. Who in your life needs to know that God has chosen them to be his very own? How might it look to share this glorious news with them?

- How do you think it would impact people in your life if they knew that God loves them with the same love he has for his Son?

- What does 1:11–13 say about God's heart for everyone? How should this guide you in sharing God's heart?

CONSIDER THIS

The refrain of our opening hymn perfectly captures the revelation-insights of our first lesson on Ephesians: "Precious, more precious; Wealth that can never be told! Oh, the unsearchable riches of Christ! Precious, more precious than gold."[2] These precious, unsearchable love gifts from the storehouses of heaven have already been lavished on us! And God is good to give them to those who ask with a sincere hunger for more.

---

2. Ibid.

Lesson 2

Explore and Experience Heaven's Riches

EPHESIANS 1:15–23

*I pray continually that the Father of Glory, the God
of our Lord Jesus Christ, would unveil in you the riches of
the Spirit of wisdom and the Spirit of revelation through your
deepening intimacy with him. (Ephesians 1:16–17)*

In the last lesson, we were given revelation-insight that the storehouses of heaven have already been opened up to us; the unsearchable, lavish love gifts of heaven are ours. But let's be honest: sometimes it doesn't feel that way. We feel defeated by the cares of this life, shamed by the sins of our past, guilty for not measuring up to God's standard. That's why we need today's lesson!

Paul recognized that the Ephesian believers felt the same way, which is why he prayed that Abba Father would impart to them in greater measure the revelation-knowledge of himself that comes through intimate relationship. He prayed that they might explore in deeper ways the glorious hope to which they'd been beckoned and wooed. He also prayed that they would experience the mighty, measureless resurrection-power of God that was unleashed when he raised Christ from the dead.

Dear brother, dear sister: heaven's riches have already been lavished on you; you own the birthright to the storehouses of heaven right now. As you explore today's lesson, may you experience these gifts in greater measure— the great hope of glory!

Discover the Heart of God

- After reading Ephesians 1:15–23, what did you notice, perhaps for the first time? What questions do you have? What did you learn about the heart of God?

- What is it that Paul prayed for the Ephesian Christians? There are several mentioned in this passage, so list them.

- What is the reason God called the Ephesian believers—all believers— to himself? In what way are our lives an "advertisement" for God?

• What power was released when God raised Christ from the dead? What happened to Christ when he was raised?

• Who alone is the leader and source of everything the church needs?

Explore the Heart of God

• What does it mean to deepen our intimacy with God? What is the result?

• What is the light of God's illumination? How does it reveal the hope of glory?

- Paul spoke of the Ephesian believers exploring and experiencing the "hope of [God's] calling" and "the wealth of God's glorious inheritance" (1:18) given to believers. What is that hopeful calling? What have we inherited from God?

- Why is God's explosive and mighty resurrection-power effective now? What does Paul mean that it works through us in this life?

- What does it mean that we are Christ's body on earth? Why must we remember that Christ is the leader and source of the church?

Experience the Heart of God

- How intimate of a relationship would you say you have with God? How does that intimacy affect your experience of the heart of God? How might you experience the heart of God differently the more your intimacy grows?

- Of the riches you listed from question three in the *Explore* section, how much have you explored and experienced these riches you've inherited in Christ?

- Do you feel that you are experiencing the full, measureless resurrection-power of Christ made available to you through faith? Explain.

- How does it impact your experience of the heart of God that Jesus has been gloriously exalted above all? How should this affect your life?

Share the Heart of God

- Why are all of the riches of God's wealth such good news to those with whom you share the heart of God?

- How might it look in your life if you were an advertisement for God's resurrection-power? How would that impact the way you share the heart of God?

- What significance is there that Christ is exalted above everything when it comes to sharing the heart of God?

- Paul said the church is Christ's body on earth; his presence flows through us in our world! What does that mean, and why is it significant for how you share the heart of God?

CONSIDER THIS

The prayer of this lesson for you is the same one Paul prayed for the Ephesian believers: May you dive deep in exploring the riches of your glorious inheritance, lavished on God's holy ones. May you experience a greater intimacy with your Abba through exploring the greater revelation-knowledge of the heart of God.

Lesson 3

Saved by the Crazy Love of God

EPHESIANS 2:1–10

For it was only through this wonderful grace that we believed in him. Nothing we did could ever earn this salvation, for it was the gracious gift from God that brought us to Christ! So no one will ever be able to boast, for salvation is never a reward for good works or human striving. (Ephesians 2:8–9)

Grace. What a crazy idea! In order to fully grasp the concept, we need to place it alongside two other words: justice and mercy. Justice is getting what we deserve, like having a license suspended after we've driven while intoxicated. Mercy is *not* getting what we deserve.

Grace, on the other hand, is when we get what we don't deserve — like driving while intoxicated, then having our DWI record wiped clean and also getting a new Ferrari. That would make absolutely no sense. And neither does God's crazy love. Think about it: every one of us was a sick drunk, intoxicated by the sins of this world, obeying every impulse. Actually, it's worse than that. In this lesson, Paul reveals that "you were once like corpses, dead in your sins and offenses" (2:1).

This is where God's crazy love comes into play. Because even though we were all the walking dead, God "united us into the very life of Christ and saved us by his wonderful grace!" (2:5). What's even more remarkable is *how* we get that grace—which today's lesson reveals in a remarkable revelation-truth.

Discover the Heart of God

- After reading Ephesians 2:1–10, what did you notice, perhaps for the first time? What questions do you have? What did you learn about the heart of God?

- What did Paul say we were once like? To what does he compare us?

- How did the "corruption that was in us from birth" (2:3) express itself? How did we live as a result? Despite being "dead and doomed in our many sins" (2:5), how did God respond?

- What did Paul say we will be throughout the coming ages?

- What was it that brought us to Christ and into a relationship with him? What separated us from him?

- As a result of our salvation, what have we become? What did God plan for us even before we were born?

Explore the Heart of God

- Why were we all once like corpses, dead in our sins and offenses? What made us this way?

- What did Paul mean when he said this corruption was in us from birth? How so, and how was this expressed in our lives? What does it tell us about the heart of God that, while we were "dead and doomed in our sins" (2:5), he still loved us?

- What did Paul mean when he said that God has "united us into the very life of Christ" and "raised us up with Christ" (2:5–6)? How has he done this?

- Read 2:8–9 again. What does this tell us about how we are saved? And how we are *not* saved? What does it tell us about the heart of God?

- Paul said, "Even before we were born, God planned in advance our destiny and the good works we would do to fulfill it!" (2:10). Although implied, these good works make up our destiny. As we yield to God, our prearranged destiny comes to pass and we are rewarded for simply doing what he wanted us to accomplish. What is that destiny? What are those works?

Experience the Heart of God

- What from your past is evidence that at one point you were dead in your sins? How did you obey the dark rulers of the earthly realm and live according to the cravings of the self-centered life?

- Paul made the point that the Ephesian Christians were once this way (just as we are). But now, because of God's love in Christ, they were (and we are) different. Was there an event in your past that united your life with Christ and raised you up with him? Describe the "before" and "after" of your life that Paul speaks of here.

- In your experience with the heart of God, how can you, right now, visibly display "the infinite, limitless riches of his grace and kindness" (2:7) that is showered on you in Jesus Christ?

- Do you ever feel that you need to work to earn God's love and salvation, and make yourself right with him? How should 2:8–9 impact your experience of the heart of God?

- What is your boast when it comes to your experience of the heart of God in salvation? Do you boast in Christ and his finished work on the cross, or in your own works and religious deeds?

Share the Heart of God

- Whom do you know who is still "dead in their sins and offenses"? How might they react to know that despite this, God still loves them?

- When sharing the heart of God, why does it matter that people understand that from birth, we are corrupt, dead, and doomed?

- Paul explains that it is by grace we are saved through faith in Christ. This means we don't have to work for it! Why is this such a powerful, freeing statement when sharing the heart of God?

- Why is 2:10 such good news for those with whom we might share the heart of God? How might it change their perspective on who God is and who they can become?

CONSIDER THIS

Paul said that we've all lived "as rebellious children subject to God's wrath ... but ..." (Praise God, there's a *but*!) "God still loved us with such great love" (2:3–4). Perhaps God's crazy love is best explained by this old hymn: "Sin and despair, like the sea waves cold; threaten the soul with infinite loss; grace that is greater, yes, grace untold; points to the refuge, the mighty cross."[3]

---

3. Julia H. Johnston, "Grace Greater Than Our Sin," 1911, public domain.

Lesson 4

Tear Down the Wall of Ethnic and Religious Separation

EPHESIANS 2:11–22

Our reconciling "Peace" is Jesus! He has made Jew and non-Jew
one in Christ. By dying as our sacrifice, he has broken down every
wall of prejudice that separated us and has now made us equal
through our union with Christ. (Ephesians 2:14)

During one of the more heated confrontations of the Cold War, US President Ronald Regan famously appealed to Soviet Union leader Mikhail Gorbachev, "Tear down this wall!" He was referring to the wall dividing West and East Berlin in Germany. In many ways, Jesus said the same about the dividing wall separating Jew from non-Jew.

The wall Paul spoke of was the ethnic and religious wall separating the nation of Israel from everybody else.[4] While God chose Israel to be a blessing to the nations (see Genesis 12:1–3), they also enjoyed special privileges

---

4   Paul probably had two "dividing walls" in mind in Ephesians 2: a metaphorical wall represented by Torah and the laws that created ethnic boundary markers, such as the purity regulations and circumcision, and the literal wall surrounding the inner courts of the Temple that religiously separated the court of the Gentiles from the court of the Israelites and divided their worship of God.

as the people of God. Yet Paul reveals something remarkable in this lesson: through the finished work of Christ, the heavenly riches Israel enjoyed became available to everyone. The ethnic and religious boundary markers (such as circumcision and food laws) that divided Israel from others have been broken down! So much so that God now sees no distinction between the Jew and the non-Jew.

As a result, we discover something even more remarkable than a torndown wall. God is now building us up "into the Holy of Holies, his dwelling place, through the power of the Holy Spirit living in you!" (2:22).

Discover the Heart of God

• After reading Ephesians 2:11–22, what did you notice, perhaps for the first time? What questions do you have? What did you learn about the heart of God?

• Paul encouraged the Ephesian believers, "Don't forget how far you've come" (2:11). How does he describe where they'd come from?

• Why were the Ephesian believers complete in Jesus Christ? What made them complete? What was the result?

- Why, in Christ, is there no more ethnic hatred between Jews and non-Jews? As a result, what has been formed?

- Even though most of us are non-Jews, like the Ephesian believers, what aren't we in Christ? What are we instead? What do we have as a result?

- How is Jesus Christ described in 2:20–22? What are we in relationship to this description? What is God transforming us into?

Explore the Heart of God

- Why do you think Paul instructed the Ephesian believers not to forget how far they had come? From where had they come, and where were they going?

• In what way is everything new for those of us who are in Christ? How is he "our reconciling 'Peace'" (2:14)?

• Paul said that Jesus has "broken down every wall of prejudice that separated us and has now made us equal through our union with Christ" (2:14). What did he mean by this? Why was there a wall, and why is it significant that it has been dissolved?

• Paul revealed that Jews and non-Jews have been united with Christ and with one another. Now we both have "equal and direct access in the realm of the Holy Spirit to come before the Father!" (2:18). What does he mean by this and why is it significant?

- What did Paul mean when he said we are like "perfectly fitted stones of the temple" (2:20)? How does the rest of 2:20 relate to this and connect? How is God "transforming each one of you into the Holy of Holies" (2:22), and how does this look in our practical lives?

Experience the Heart of God

- Sometimes in the Christian life, it's easy to do exactly what Paul warns against: we forget how far we've come in our new life! Spend some time taking stock in your experience of the heart of God. Remind yourself who you were and who you are now in Christ.

- What does it mean to you that "although you were once distant and far away from God, now you have been brought delightfully close to him" (2:13)? How should this realization impact your experience of the heart of God every day?

- In Christ, there is no such thing as ethnic separation. They have been dissolved by Christ's crucifixion so that we are all united together in Christ. What ways can you show this to be true in your own Christian community?

- Do you live with God the Father as if you had direct access to him by the Holy Spirit? Explain.

Share the Heart of God

- Paul reminded us that because of Christ, "Everything is new!" (2:13). How should this newness be at the core of how you share the heart of God?

- Paul tells a story in 2:13 that summarizes our spiritual journey. Why is this story so key to sharing the heart of God with others?

- The Christian faith offers something unique to other faiths: equal and direct access to God. How might this be good news for people you know?

- Paul likens the church to a building, a temple of perfectly fitted stones with Christ as the cornerstone. How should this realization impact our love for fellow believers? How about our witness to the world?

CONSIDER THIS

Just as the Cold War was fraught with heated confrontations that brought out sharp nationalistic divisions between the East and West, our day is one of ethnic and religious divisions—even inside the church. May we remember that any and all walls of ethnic and denominational hatred have been obliterated through the crucifixion. May we work toward being built up in unity as a beautiful dwelling of God!

Lesson 5

God's Secret Revealed

EPHESIANS 3:1–13

There has never been a generation that has been given the detailed understanding of this glorious and divine mystery until now. He kept it a secret until this generation. God is revealing it only now to his sacred apostles and prophets by the Holy Spirit.
(Ephesians 3:5)

If you know anything about the days of pirates and buccaneers, you know that on hundreds of maps, a big black X marked the spot to secret buried treasure. In today's lesson, Paul describes a secret treasure revealed to him by another map—direct divine revelation.

Paul's treasure was found in the mystery about the Messiah, and the map was the gospel. As Paul revealed, there had never been a generation that had been given the full map to understanding this glorious, divine mystery. God had kept it a secret until the time of Paul and was unveiling it through the gospel. This mystery of Christ leads to the salvation of both Jews and non-Jews and their mutual inheritance in the promises of God.

In Christ is found the most precious of buried treasure—the riches of heaven we've discovered and explored in the past few lessons. And the big black X on the map leading to the riches is the grace of God. God's love plan unveils before us his full and diverse wisdom so that we can access the riches of Christ—both now and forevermore!

Discover the Heart of God

- After reading Ephesians 3:1–13, what did you notice, perhaps for the first time? What questions do you have? What did you learn about the heart of God?

- What had happened to Paul because of his love for Christ? Why did this happen?

- What had the generation of Ephesian believers been given that other generations hadn't?

- What empowered Paul to boldly preach God's message to non-Jewish people? What did he share?

- What plan was destined from the eternal ages and fulfilled in Christ? List all that we've received through this plan.

Explore the Heart of God

- What did Paul mean when he said that he was made Christ's prisoner for the sake of the Ephesian believers? What might this reveal about the heart of God?

• Paul said he received "divine revelation," which became a letter he wrote to the Ephesian believers. It was then preserved for us in what we know as the book of Ephesians. What might this tell us about the Scriptures and the heart of God?

• Why was it significant that there had "never been a generation that has been given the detailed understanding of this glorious and divine mystery until now" (3:5)? Why had God not revealed it to previous generations? Why did He reveal it "now"?

• The word *unfading* in 3:8 comes from an Aramaic word that can also be translated "unquestionable" or "without fault." The Greek uses the word *unsearchable*. What are the "unfading, inexhaustible riches of Christ" (3:8)?

- What does it tell you about the heart of God that his plan for the church was "destined from eternal ages" (3:11)?

Experience the Heart of God

- Paul's imprisonment for the sake of sharing the grace-gospel reminds us of all the people God has used to carry his message along. Consider these people and thank God for them.

- How might 3:1–4 teach us about how God uses circumstances for his glory and the good of others? How should it impact how we experience the heart of God?

- As believers living nearly two thousand years after Christ, we know the secret God kept from other generations that has been graciously revealed to us. Spend time thanking him for revealing the wonderful mysteries and grace of Christ to you, as he did to Paul.

- Paul said that because of Christ, "we have boldness through him, and free access as kings before the Father because of our complete confidence in Christ's faithfulness" (3:12). How should this realization impact how we experience the heart of God?

Share the Heart of God

- Have you ever suffered for the sake of sharing the heart of God with others? If so, what was that like? If not, how might it look in your life to be "imprisoned" for the sake of the grace-gospel?

- Paul said that he shared with the non-Jewish people "the unfading, inexhaustible riches of Christ" (3:8). What are these riches that you can share with those you know?

- Paul said God's grace alone empowered him to boldly share the heart of God. It's what he leaned on. What do you lean on? What empowers you? What fuels your passion for sharing the heart of God?

CONSIDER THIS

In the case of the gospel, grace marks the spot! It empowers us to find God's secret plan to rescue us and re-create the world in Christ. Thanks to this grace, we have access to the "inexhaustible riches of Christ, which are beyond comprehension" (3:8). May we join Paul in sharing with others the secret that's been revealed to us, the treasures we have discovered and experienced so joyfully.

Lesson 6

Christ's Multidimensional, Magnificent Love

EPHESIANS 3:14–21

How deeply intimate and far-reaching is his love! How endur-
ing and inclusive it is! Endless love beyond measurement that
transcends our understanding—this extravagant love pours into
you until you are filled to overflowing with the fullness of God!
(Ephesians 3:19)

On January 26, 1905, the Cullinan Diamond, a 3,106-carat jewel, was unearthed in South Africa. Weighing 1.37 pounds, it was later featured among the British crown jewels and is considered one of our world's greatest treasures. But this earthly treasure pales in comparison to the crown jewel of the vast storehouse of heaven—the three-word treasure that defines the essence of our heavenly riches:

God loves you.

Reread those words. Then read them again, because this gift has been lavished upon us by our heavenly Father! And Paul reminds us today of its multidimensionality and magnificence. He does so by describing its vastness and greatness, its depth and reach.

"How deeply intimate and far-reaching is his love! How enduring and inclusive it is! Endless love beyond measurement that transcends our understanding—this extravagant love pours into you until you are filled to overflowing with the fullness of God!" (4:18–19).

There has never been uttered a three-word sentence in any language with as much depth and magnitude as "God loves you." It's so simple, yet so profound. So familiar, yet so mind-blowing! May you walk away from today's lesson with a greater appreciation for and deeper revelation-understanding of Christ's multidimensional, magnificent love for you.

Discover the Heart of God

- After reading Ephesians 3:14–21, what did you notice, perhaps for the first time? What questions do you have? What did you learn about the heart of God?

- What did Paul do when he thought about the wisdom of God's plan?

- What provides us with a secure foundation that "grows and grows"? What happens as our spiritual strength increases?

- Describe the "astonishing love of Christ in all its dimensions" (3:18–19).

- What did Paul encourage us to never doubt?

- How much did Paul promise God would achieve on our behalf? What will his mighty power do for us?

Explore the Heart of God

- Paul said that when he thought about the wisdom of God's plan, he knelt in humble awe. To what "plan" was Paul referring?

- What do you think are the "unlimited riches of [God's] glory and favor" that Paul referenced in 3:16? Why is this an appropriate thing to pray for?

- How does Christ's love—"the very source and root of your life" (3:17)—provide us with a secure, growing foundation?

- Read 3:18–19 again. What does this description of God's love tell us about his heart toward us?

- Why don't we ever need to doubt God's mighty power to work in us and to accomplish all that he will achieve in us?

Experience the Heart of God

- What has been your response to the wisdom of God's grace-gospel plan in Jesus Christ? Humility and awe, like Paul? Or something else?

- How have you experienced the outpouring of the unlimited riches of God's glory and favor in your life?

- How has the love of Christ provided you with a secure foundation for growing as a person and Christian as you've experienced the heart of God?

- How have you personally experienced the "deeply intimate and far-reaching," "enduring and inclusive" love of God (3:18–19)? Share a specific story that illustrates your experience of God's heart.

- Paul told us to never doubt God's mighty power at work in our lives. Do you doubt that power? If so, why do you think that is? How should 3:20 encourage your experience of the heart of God?

Share the Heart of God

- Who do you want God to "pour out over you the unlimited riches of his glory and favor" (3:16)?

- What does 3:18–20 tell us about the heart of God for people, and how can we better share and show this to those we know?

- If 3:18–19 is a description of God's love for people, how should our lives reflect this love, especially as we share the heart of God?

- Not only does God work on our behalf, he is also able to accomplish more for other people than we could imagine. Whom do you know who needs God to "achieve infinitely more than your greatest request, your most unbelievable dream, and your wildest imagination" (3:20)? Spend time praying for this request, believing God's power will accomplish it.

CONSIDER THIS

Don't ever doubt the truth of God's love for you and the power of his love working in you. This love will accomplish infinitely more than you could ever dream. Our only response is to offer what Paul offered: "all the glorious praise that rises from every church in every generation through Jesus Christ—and all that will yet be manifest through time and eternity. Amen!" (3:21).

Lesson 7

———

The Body of Christ Built Up

EPHESIANS 4:1–16

*Every member has been given divine gifts to contribute to the
growth of all; and as these gifts operate effectively throughout
the whole body, we are built up and made perfect in love.*
(Ephesians 4:16)

The human body is a wonderful gift! Consider the sweet melodies our
ears allow us to enjoy; the myriad things we can experience because of our
two hands and feet. The body truly is a wonderful gift—when its members
are working well and working together. Anyone who has lost his or her mo-
bility knows that paralysis grinds life to a halt. The same is true of the body
of Christ, the church.

In today's lesson, Paul reminds us that Christians joined together in
community are part of heaven's riches given to the church. He identifies
several of these human grace-gifts: apostles, prophets, evangelists, pastors,
and teachers. We are gifts to one another, given by the Lord God to serve
and build up the body of Christ and bring it to perfection. But only if we
faithfully "guard the sweet harmony of the Holy Spirit among [us] in the
bonds of peace" (4:3).

The fullness of maturity and perfection cannot come to the body of

Christ without the example and teaching of these five ministries. Keep reading to learn how to appreciate them for the grace-gifts they are!

Discover the Heart of God

- After reading Ephesians 4:1–16, what did you notice, perhaps for the first time? What questions do you have? What did you learn about the heart of God?

- What was Paul's plea to the Ephesian Christians?

- What does Paul encourage us to faithfully guard? Why did he encourage this?

- Christ has appointed believers to a number of roles within the church. What are they? Why does he appoint people to these roles? What is their calling? At what point will their grace ministries cease to function?

- What will we become when we are spiritually mature and fully developed in the abundance of Christ?

Explore the Heart of God

- What does it mean to walk in a way that's "suitable to your high rank, given to you in your divine calling" (4:1)?

- Why does Paul want us to "guard the sweet harmony" among us and "be one body and one spirit" (4:3, 4)? What does this create?

- What does Paul mean by "we share in one faith, one baptism, and one Father" (4:5)?

- What is the significance of Paul quoting Psalm 68:18 in connection with the work of Christ in 4:8?

- Paul said Christ gave to the church apostles, prophets, evangelists, pastors, and teachers. What is the significance of each of these roles in the body of Christ, and what is their collective role? How does the church benefit from their ministries?

Experience the Heart of God

- How are you walking? Is it in a way that's suitable or unsuitable to your high rank and divine calling?

- In 4:3–4 Paul described an intentional pursuit of Christian unity. How would such a Christian pursuit impact your experience of the heart of God? How might it look in your life to pursue it?

- Paul explained that all Christians have a common faith, baptism, and Father. Why is this significant to your experience of the heart of God? How do you experience this oneness in your life?

- Are you among those who've been given a special grace ministry to serve the church? How can you use that calling "to nurture and prepare all the holy believers to do their own works of ministry" (4:12)? If not one of those five, what other "divine gift" have you been given "to contribute to the growth of all" (4:16)?

Share the Heart of God

- How might how your walk as a Christian—whether suitably or unsuitably—impact the way you share the heart of God?

- Why is "guarding the sweet harmony" and being "one body and one spirit" so important when sharing the heart of God? What does it show? What does it prove?

- In what way is the declaration Paul makes from Psalm 68:18 an important part of sharing the heart of God? What does it tell our friends and neighbors?

- If you've been given the grace to be an apostle, prophet, evangelist, pastor, or teacher, how is this gift a crucial one for the church's mission to share the heart of God and the story of Christ?

CONSIDER THIS

Anyone who has had a serious injury or illness knows that when the parts of our human bodies function in harmony, as they were appointed to, marvelous things happen. But when they don't, pain and misery result. May we rejoice in the riches we find in the body's grace-gifts. May we also guard the sweet harmony of that body so that we will be one—just as we were called to be.

Lesson 8

Put Off Your Old Self, Put On Your New Christ-Within Life

EPHESIANS 4:17–32

He has taught you to let go of the lifestyle of the ancient man,
the old self-life, which was corrupted by sinful and deceitful
desires that spring from delusions. Now it's time to be made new
by every revelation that's been given to you.
(Ephesians 4:22–23)

Imagine a homeless person in Washington DC being invited to live in the White House. This person is offered all of the comfort, security, riches, and satisfaction the president and first family enjoy. But he or she rejects the invitation, preferring instead to live on the streets. Ludicrous, right?

Yet don't we make the same choice when we live like unbelievers, clinging to life in this world? That's what Paul addresses in today's lesson: letting go of the old self-life to embrace the glorious Christ-within life as our new life. This kind of life contrasts sharply with unbelievers, "who walk in their empty delusions," "are so far from God," and have "cut themselves off from their only true hope" (4:17–19). Instead, the way of Christ lets go of dishonesty, anger, and stealing; it encourages and graciously forgives others.

As we've already discovered, we were once as hopeless and destitute as someone living life on the streets. But because of God's crazy love, we've been made alive in Christ and have been given the riches of heaven. So let's listen to Paul and put off our old self, then put on our new life—the Christ-within life!

Discover the Heart of God

- After reading Ephesians 4:17–32, what did you notice, perhaps for the first time? What questions do you have? What did you learn about the heart of God?

- Why is the logic of unbelievers so corrupted and clouded? To what has that led, and what has been the result?

- What did Paul say is "embodied in Jesus" (4:21)? What has Jesus taught us about life and how to live?

- How does Paul say we are "made new" and "transformed"?

- What did Paul say God has done for us that we should also do for others?

Explore the Heart of God

- What is the result of unbelievers being far from God? How has their "moral darkness" (4:18) kept them from knowing God?

- What is the way of life Christ has unfolded within us? How is it so different from the way of life for unbelievers?

- Paul said Christ has taught us to let go of the self-absorbed lifestyle. What is that lifestyle? What has he called us to instead?

- How do you think it looks and what does it mean to grieve the Spirit of God or take for granted his holy influence?

- At the end of this reading, Paul linked God's forgiveness of us to our forgiveness of others. Why?

Experience the Heart of God

- Paul encouraged us not to live like the unbelievers around us. How would that look in your life if you followed his encouragement? What "empty delusions," "corrupted logic," and "spiritual apathy" exist around you that you need to guard against to fully experience the heart of God?

- Paul believed that in Christ, we are taught to let go and be transformed by embracing and putting on the Christ-within life. What do you need to let go of in order to fully embrace this new life God has for you, flowing from his heart to yours?

- Do you ever grieve or take advantage of the Holy Spirit? Take time to consider Paul's words in 4:30, and seek repentance if need be.

• How might you experience God's heart more fully by forgiving others in your life as God has forgiven you?

Share the Heart of God

• Paul revealed the lifestyle of unbelievers around us as full of "empty delusions," "corrupt logic," and "spiritual apathy." How might the way you love be a way to share the heart of God with those whose hearts are far from him?

• The truth about ultimate reality—the way God intended for us to live—is embodied in Jesus. This means that sharing him by modeling him is a good way to share the heart of God! Who in your life needs to know how God intends for them to live? How might that look to share his intent with that person?

- Paul encouraged us to "guard your speech" by never letting "ugly or hateful words come from your mouth" (4:29). Ask God to help you not let any unwholesome talk come from your mouth so that you can share the heart of God.

- We are called to share the heart of God with those around us in one of the most difficult ways: forgiveness. Is there anyone you need to forgive as God has forgiven you?

CONSIDER THIS

Why would we scramble for scraps off the table of this unbelieving world when we've been lavishly gifted with all the riches of heaven? Let us cast off the old self-life and let God re-create within us the new Christ-within life, making the truths of the Anointed One and his heavenly riches manifest for all the world to see!

Lesson 9

Be Very Careful How You Live

EPHESIANS 5:1–20

So be very careful how you live, not being foolish as those with no understanding, but live honorably with true wisdom, for we are living in evil times. Take full advantage of every day as you spend your life for his purposes. (Ephesians 5:15–16)

There's a childhood song that reflects today's reading in Ephesians. The song encourages young people (and the young at heart) to be careful about what they see, hear, do, and say, and where they go. Why? Because our Father up above is looking down in love. So be careful, little eyes, ears, hands, mouths, and feet!

Paul has a similar message for us. We're encouraged to take great care in how we live our lives as adults—what we see and say, what we do, and where we go. Why? Not just because our Father is looking down on us, there's more. "Once your life was full of sin's darkness, but now you have the very light of our Lord shining through you because of your union with him" (5:8). Once we walked in sexual immorality, but now we should let the light of purity shine through us. Once we talked with obscenities and worthless insults, but now we should let the light of worship flood out of us.

Paul invites us to be filled with the fullness of the Holy Spirit so that our life-song will overflow with joyous music to the Lord Jehovah!

Discover the Heart of God

- After reading Ephesians 5:1–20, what did you notice, perhaps for the first time? What questions do you have? What did you learn about the heart of God?

- What did Christ do on our behalf? How does this reflect the heart of God?

- Paul had strong words of warning against sexual immorality. What are those words? Why did he instruct with them?

• Who should we be careful never to listen to?

• Paul described two states of our lives: *before* and *after* our union with Christ. Describe these two states. What is the mission Paul says we've been given in light of this union, and how should this union affect our mission?

• Whom are we never to associate ourselves with? Why not, and what should we do instead?

Explore the Heart of God

- How do you think it looks to "follow God and imitate all he does in everything you do" (5:1)? In what way is Christ's love "extravagant" (5:2)? How should that love compel us to walk?

- How is Paul's instruction to "guard your speech" connected to his encouragement to "let worship fill your heart" and give thanksgiving to God (5:4)?

- Why is greed the essence of idolatry? Why can't greedy people inherit the kingdom of God?

- In what way were we all once "full of sin's darkness" (5:8)? How does it look to live as children of light, letting the benefits of that light be evident in our lives?

- What did Paul mean when he said, "Whatever the revelation-light exposes, it will also correct, and everything that reveals truth is light to the soul" (5:13)? How does this happen?

- How does Paul's quote of Isaiah in 5:14 relate to our mission of living as children of light?

Experience the Heart of God

- What does it say to you about the extravagant love of God that Christ "surrendered his life as a sacrifice" for you (5:2)? How can you live in response?

- In 5:3–4, Paul listed a number of ways of living: sexual immorality, lust, greed, obscene talk, and worthless insults. Are you living with these in your life? If any are a struggle for you, ask God to help you have nothing to do with them.

- In what ways has your life been "full of sin's darkness"? How can you "live as children flooded with his revelation-light" (5:8)? How would such living impact your experience of the heart of God?

- How carefully are you living? Are you being foolish or living honorably (5:15–16)?

Share the Heart of God

- How do you think following God and imitating all he does would impact how you share the heart of God?

- Sometimes we can be careless with our speech, but Paul instructed us to take care and replace obscenities and foolish talk with worship. Why might this matter so much when sharing the heart of God?

- In what ways can you live as a child of light for the sake of those around you who need to personally experience the heart of God? How might such living expose, correct, and reveal truth (5:13)?

- Why is being careful how we live and living "honorably with true wisdom" in these evil times so important when it comes to sharing the heart of God (5:16)? Why is what Paul encourages in 5:19–20 so important?

CONSIDER THIS

As the song goes, be careful what you see and say, what you do, and where you go; be careful how you live and love! Not only because we represent God as his dearly loved children, but because Christ loved us by surrendering himself as a sacrifice for us. How else could we live than "to learn to choose what is beautiful to our Lord" (5:10)?

A Lesson on Tender Devotion, Part 1

EPHESIANS 5:21–33

And you honor Christ by yielding to one another. Be tenderly devoted to each other in love. (Ephesians 5:21)

Sadly, marriage in the West seems to be on its last leg. That shouldn't be any surprise given the level of divorce and redefinition that plagues much of our culture. And yet God loves marriage! After all, he designed it and gifted it to us for our enjoyment and prosperity. But we need a fresh vision for this holy institution and sacrament. Paul offers such a vision.

In the longest passage in the New Testament about husbands and wives, Paul offers an important revelation-truth that's necessary for all of our relationships, but especially our marital ones. Tender devotion flows from honoring Christ. Wives love, respond to, and devote themselves to their husbands when their love, response, and devotion is for the Lord. Husbands love, lead, and care for their wives best when they mirror the way Christ loves, leads, and cares for his own Bride, the church.

It's no wonder that 53 percent of happily married couples say, "God is at the center of our marriage," while 30 percent of struggling couples say he isn't.[5] Why? Because when Christ and his vision of tender devotion are at the center of marriages, they flourish!

Discover the Heart of God

- After reading Ephesians 5:21–33, what did you notice, perhaps for the first time? What questions do you have? What did you learn about the heart of God?

- How does Paul say we honor Christ in our day-to-day lives?

- How are wives and husbands called to yield to each other? How are they to be tenderly devoted to each other? To what did Paul compare their devotion and love?

---

5   Shaunti Feldhahn, *The Surprising Secrets of Highly Happy Marriages* (Colorado Springs: Multnomah, 2013), 179.

- In what way do husbands have the obligation to love and care for their wives?

- What did Christ do for his body, the members who make up "his flesh and bones" (5:30)?

Explore the Heart of God

- How is it that we "honor Christ" when we yield to one another and devote ourselves to each other? How is this true, specifically in marriage relationships?

- What's the relationship between wives being tenderly devoted to their husbands and to Christ?

- How is a husband's demonstration of love for his wife the same as, and related to, Christ's demonstration of love for us? Explain how a husband's actions toward his wife are related to and are supposed to mirror Christ's actions toward his Bride.

- Paul related the care husbands have for themselves to their care of their wives. Explain what Paul meant by this.

- How is 5:31–32 one of the most important and beautiful definitions of marriage in Scripture? How does it compare and contrast to our society's definition?

- How is 5:33 related to Jesus' greatest commandment? How should that commandment guide our marriages?

Experience the Heart of God

- Who in your life do you need to yield to and be tenderly devoted to in order to honor Christ?

- If you are a wife, how does 5:22–24 speak to how you need to treat your husband? How would following these instructions deepen your experience of the heart of God?

- If you are a husband, how does 5:25–30 speak to how you need to treat your wife? How would following these instructions deepen your experience of the heart of God?

- The Greek word for "radiance" (*endoxos*) in 5:27 can also mean "gorgeous, honorable, esteemed, splendid, infused with glory." This is what Christ's love will do to you. How have you experienced this love yourself?

- How should 5:31–32 guide our understanding of marriage? How does it draw us deeper into the heart of God?

Share the Heart of God

- Whom do you know who needs to hear 5:22–30? How might sharing it with them draw them closer to the heart of God?

- The definition of marriage Paul quotes from Genesis 2:24 and further defines in Ephesians 5:31–32 is countercultural. Why might sharing it and standing for it be a way to share the heart of God?

- If you are married, how can following Paul's charge in 5:33 be a practical way to share the heart of God with those you know?

CONSIDER THIS

Imagine if everyone in the church took Paul's lesson on marital devotion seriously. Wives would feel loved; husbands would love well. Husbands would lead like Christ; wives would respond as unto Christ. Wives would experience the utmost care; husbands would experience tender devotion. In other words, husbands and wives would experience the depths of the heart of God as he expresses it toward his children!

Lesson 11

A Lesson on Tender Devotion, Part 2

EPHESIANS 6:1–9

*Be assured that anything you do that is beautiful
and excellent will be repaid by our Lord, whether you are
an employee or an employer. (Ephesians 6:8)*

If you thought you were off the hook in the last lesson because you aren't married, you're out of luck! Paul continues his lesson on tender devotion by addressing three more relationships: children to parents, employees to employers, and leaders to followers.

He begins by reminding his readers of one of God's most important commands: "Honor your father and your mother" (6:2). While we might think this command applies only to the eighteen-and-under crowd, it was meant for adult children of older parents as much as younger ones. And then there is the relationship that governs our nine-to-five lives: the employee-employer relationship. Paul has important words for us as we work for and serve our employers, as well as for those who lead and manage. Words like *listen, obey, serve,* and *caretake*.

Christians in Paul's day would have been asking the same questions we ask in ours: "What does it mean to live out my role in society as a Christian child, employee, and leader?" One thing defines these roles: the lordship of Christ. This lesson will teach us how to do our Master's will by honoring our parents, our bosses, and our followers as servants of Christ.

Discover the Heart of God

- After reading Ephesians 6:1–9, what did you notice, perhaps for the first time? What questions do you have? What did you learn about the heart of God?

- Paul continued his theme of tender devotion from 5:21 with his words in 6:1–9. Who did he address this time?

- What should children do if they want to be wise? What does the Bible promise children who respond this way?

• What should fathers be careful not to do? What should they do instead?

• What are employees called to do, and what did Paul promise employees who respond in this way? How should "caretakers of the flock" (6:9)—whether in church or work leadership—behave with those they oversee?

Explore the Heart of God

• In what way are each of these relationships in 6:1–9 (and also 5:22–33) a way we "honor Christ by yielding to one another" from Paul's instructions in 5:21?

• Why do you think God connects wisdom and prosperity to children obeying and honoring their parents? What does this reveal about the heart of God?

• How do you think it looks when fathers "exasperate" their children? How does it look to "raise them up with loving discipline and counsel that brings the revelation of our Lord" (6:4)?

• How do employees and employers each reflect the heart of God when they follow Paul's instructions in 6:5–8?

• In what ways does God repay employees and employers for beautiful, excellent work?

Experience the Heart of God

- While you may no longer be a child, you are still someone's son or daughter. How might it look to live out God's command to "honor your father and your mother"—considering it was given to adults as much as to children?

- Do you have any personal experience with being "exasperated ... to anger" by a parent? If so, what was that like? If you are a parent, consider how you treat your children—whether you exasperate or encourage them—and how you can teach them the ways of the Lord.

- Read 6:5–8 again. How would it look in your work life to live out these teachings? How would doing so draw you into the heart of God?

- While we may not always believe it, work is a good thing. We were created to work; and God promises to bless and repay our beautiful, excellent work. How does this knowledge from 6:8 deepen your understanding and help you experience of the heart of God?

Share the Heart of God

- Consider your parents. How can you share the heart of God with them by honoring them as God has commanded you?

- Parents, consider your children. How can you share and show the heart of God by "[raising] them up with loving discipline and counsel that brings the revelation of our Lord" (6:4)?

- Paul's encouragement to work for our employers "as though you were working for the Master" (6:5) is convicting! Think about your own job. Is this how you work? How can you share the heart of God with your boss and employer by living out these words?

- In 6:9 Paul closes our reading by issuing a challenge to "caretakers of the flock," which can refer to leadership both in the church and in the workplace. If you are such a person, how can you extend God's forgiveness and guard against favoritism?

CONSIDER THIS

As Christians, the lordship of Christ should impact every one of our roles in day-to-day life. Whether you are a teenager or an adult child of aging parents, a fast-food worker at a local restaurant or an employee of a multinational corporation, a small-business owner or a Fortune 500 CEO—we honor our Master by honoring, listening to, and serving others with tender devotion.

Lesson 12

The Gift of God's Full Suit of Armor

EPHESIANS 6:10–24

Put on the full suit of armor that God wears when he goes into battle, so that you will be protected as you fight against the evil strategies of the accuser! (Ephesians 6:11)

Imagine walking into a battle with a fire-breathing dragon wearing nothing more than a T-shirt and sweatpants, wielding nothing more than a spatula in one hand and a paper plate in the other. Foolish wouldn't begin to describe it! Yet isn't that how many of us walk into battle every day with our fire-breathing accuser?

We forget that our hand-to-hand combat isn't with our coworkers or boss, with our neighbors or family. Paul reminds us here that our daily battle is against the highest principalities and authorities of evil. This means we need to arm ourselves to the hilt! Thankfully, Paul also gives us a revelation-reminder that we have access to the riches of heaven's armory. In fact, God gives us the very same full suit of armor he himself uses when he does battle with the devil.

How could any of us expect to stand up to an opponent with sweatpants and a spatula? So put on the full armor of God, complete with a heavenly belt and breastplate, shield and sword. When we do, we will be able to stand our ground and rise victoriously!

Discover the Heart of God

- After reading Ephesians 6:10–24, what did you notice, perhaps for the first time? What questions do you have? What did you learn about the heart of God?

- What important truths did Paul save for his last lesson in Ephesians?

- What is the "full suit of armor that God wears" (6:11)? Why did Paul urge us to wear all the armor that God provides? What does it reveal about God's heart?

- List all the pieces of the armor of God we've been given, then explain how each piece benefits us if we wear it and use it.

- What did Paul urge us to do concerning our spiritual lives in his final encouragement before he closed his letter with the word he was sending with his friend Tychicus?

Explore the Heart of God

- What did Paul mean when he said that our "hand-to-hand combat is not with human beings" (6:12)? Whom do we really struggle and fight with? Why is this a significant revelation?

- What is the belt from God's armor, and how does it help us "stand in triumph" (6:14)?

- How does the protective armor benefit us? What does it cover?

- Why is faith a shield? How does it benefit our day-to-day life?

• The "sword" Paul speaks of was probably a short sword used for defense more than the long sword of offensive attack. How does this deepen your understanding of the "Spirit-sword" we've been given by God?

• Why is prayer so vital to our spiritual hand-to-hand combat?

Experience the Heart of God

• How would it look to experience the heart of God each day by standing "victorious with the force of his explosive power flowing in and through you" (6:10)?

- How much (or little) of God's armor do you wear and carry with you as you walk into your day-to-day life? Which pieces do you often wear? Which ones do you need to make a more deliberate effort to put on?

- How often do you pray? Is it an everyday part of your life, or only when you're in trouble? How would it impact your experience of the heart of God and Christian life if you constantly interceded through passionate prayer?

Share the Heart of God

- Strength and victory are two things missing from many people's lives. Yet they're what all people desire. Whom do you know who needs the supernatural strength and victory that comes through union with Christ? What could you share about what Christ offers in order to draw them closer to the heart of God?

• Sometimes we forget that our daily battles aren't with people, "but with the highest principalities and authorities operating in rebellion under the heavenly realms" (6:12). Is there anyone in your life you need to remember isn't your enemy? Spend time praying for that person and for ways to share with him or her the heart of God, instead of engaging in hand-to-hand combat.

• Paul urges us to pray passionately, constantly intercede, pray the blessings of God upon all his believers, and pray that the revelation of God's hope-filled gospel would go forth (6:18–20). Spend time doing all this as a way to share the heart of God with those you know.

CONSIDER THIS

Imagine walking into your day looking like something out of the *Braveheart* movie: wearing the trusty belt of triumphant truth; solid, holy armor covering your heart; stabilizing shoes of peace; faith's wrap-around shield; the sturdy helmet of salvation; and the mighty, razor-sharp Spirit-sword of God's Word. If that's how you armed yourself, combined with passionate prayer, the devil wouldn't stand a chance!

Encounter the Heart of God

The Passion Translation Bible is a new, heart-level translation that expresses God's fiery heart of love to this generation, using Hebrew, Greek, and Aramaic manuscripts and merging the emotion and life-changing truth of God's Word. If you are hungry for God and want to know him on a deeper level, The Passion Translation will help you encounter God's heart and discover what he has for your life.

The Passion Translation box set includes the following eight books:

Psalms: Poetry on Fire

Proverbs: Wisdom from Above

Song of Songs: Divine Romance

Matthew: Our Loving King

John: Eternal Love

Luke and Acts: To the Lovers of God

Hebrews and James: Faith Works

Letters from Heaven: From the Apostle Paul (Galatians, Ephesians, Philippians, Colossians, I & II Timothy)

Additional titles available include:

Mark: Miracles and Mercy
Romans: Grace and Glory
1 & 2 Corinthians: Love and Truth
Letters of Love: From Peter, John, and Jude (1, 2 Peter; 1, 2, 3 John; Jude)

THE
PASSION
TRANSLATION

thePassionTranslation.com